Speed Reading Revolution

Double Your Comprehension and Retention

Table of Contents

Chapter 1. Introduction

The dawn of a new era in knowledge absorption is upon us with the Speed Reading Revolution! Witness a sweeping change that is designed to effectively double your comprehension and retention in no time at all. This isn't just any concept; it's a powerful tool that is real, achievable, and transformative, bound to reshape your approach to reading and learning altogether. Our Special Report is bursting with exciting, practical techniques and expert-backed strategies to help you cruise through pages at lightning speed, without compromising on understanding or recall. This trusted guide is more than just a purchase; it's an investment towards a more informed, productive future. Dive in and turbocharge your reading skills, promising yourself the gift of time and the thrill of intellectual achievement, all packed into this special report waiting to be yours!

Chapter 2. The Genesis of Speed Reading

The fascinating journey to the era of speed reading begins with an understanding of traditional reading. The regular approach would involve reading, digesting, and understanding each word one by one, while our mind forms images, reflections, connections, and recalls related memories. However, with the regular influx of information via books, articles, emails, reports and more, our current reading approach might seem inefficient.

2.1. Recognizing the Need for Speed Reading

With the digital age taking center stage, and our lives becoming perpetually intertwined with the ever-evolving mesh of information technology, the bombardment of data on everyone's plates is more than ever before. What used to be piles upon piles of physical paperwork has now turned into an endless stream of digital data, all requiring your attention, processing, and comprehension. It is amidst this tide of relentless information deluge that the concept of speed reading emerged like a beacon of hope.

The inflection point can be traced back to the mid-20th century when Evelyn Wood, a schoolteacher from the United States, coined the term 'speed reading'. Wood's university experience, where she was overwhelmed with the amount of reading, led her to research and develop techniques to read faster. She observed a co-worker who could complete reading tasks in a fraction of the time it took her. Intrigued, she discovered that this high-speed reader did not read left-to-right, word-by-word, like most people but used her hand to guide her gaze down the center of the page, reading several lines at once.

Wood's revolutionary contribution to reading practices marked the genesis of speed reading. Many are surprised to discover that our brain has a natural capacity for processing words at a much faster rate than our traditional reading allows. It was this untapped potential that became the cornerstone of speed reading.

2.2. Foundational Techniques of Speed Reading

The fundamental ethos of speed reading lies in enhancing two key components: pace and comprehension. It is not about skipping chunks of text or merely skimming through the material. Rather, it is based on the principle of optimizing the focus and cognitive capacity of our brains, enabling us to digest larger chunks of information quickly while maintaining comprehension.

One effective and popular method to increase reading speed is 'chunking,' which involves viewing a group of words together instead of separately, thereby reducing the time spent on eye fixation. Another foundational technique is 'minimizing subvocalization.' Subvocalization refers to the voice we hear inside our heads when we read, which often slows us down to the pace of our speech. Minimizing this can dramatically improve reading speed.

Other commonly employed techniques include 'meta guiding,' where the reader uses a pointer like a finger or pen to guide their eyes while reading, and 'regression reduction', which aims to decrease unnecessary backward eye movement.

2.3. Evolution and Advent of Speed Reading Tools

Once the premise and potential of speed reading were established, it didn't take long for avid readers, entrepreneurs, and educators alike to seek ways to streamline and advance these techniques. This period saw an evolution from basic manual methods like finger-guiding and chunking words to the advent of sophisticated speed reading tools and software.

Products such as rapid serial visual presentation (RSVP), Quick Reader, and Speed Reader Enhanced have shifted from traditional printed texts to digital domains, wherein words or group of words appear in rapid succession at a designated spot on the screen, thus maximizing focus and minimizing eye movement.

Contemporary tools have also incorporated personalized adjustments for speed and difficulty level, in-text comprehension checks, progress tracking, and interactive exercises aimed at training your eye and brain muscles to process information more efficiently.

2.4. The Psychological Perspective

From a cognitive psychology viewpoint, speed reading leverages the human brain's inherent plasticity, the ability to change and adapt as a result of experience and learning. George A. Miller, a cognitive psychologist, introduced us to the millisecond magic of the human brain's working memory bandwidth or "The magical number seven, plus or minus two," stating that we can comfortably process seven chunks of information simultaneously.

By tapping into the nuances of the cognitive aspects of reading, contemporary speed reading methods also aim to improve concentration, minimize distraction, and enhance cognitive processing and memory retention.

2.5. The Future of Speed Reading

As we continue to advance in the digital era, the magnitude and complexity of information we encounter will only expand, and so will the demand for versatile and efficient reading capabilities. How we adapt to this trend will influence our efficiency and productivity significantly.

In this pursuit, we realize that the potential of speed reading extends beyond mere rapid text consumption. It leads the way to optimize our cognitive abilities, revolutionize our approach to learning, and empower ourselves to navigate an increasingly information-driven world.

The remarkable journey of speed reading, from its genesis to its current digital adaptation, underlines the persistent human endeavor to learn, improve, and adapt in an ever-evolving world. Enriched with potential, vision, and an unwavering commitment, the future of speed reading exudes an atmosphere of optimism, insight, and anticipation.

The history of speed reading is not just a tale of an improved reading technique but rather a reflection of our unending quest for knowledge, efficiency, and improvement. In its essence, the genesis of speed reading mirrors humankind's relentless pursuit to push boundaries of the possible, deconstruct and rebuild processes, and continuously evolve with time.

Chapter 3. Unveiling the Brain of a Speed Reader

To truly understand speed reading, it's essential that we delve deep into the workings of the brain and uncover the processes that make it possible. In this section, we will discover the interplay between the brain, reading, and speed.

3.1. The Brain and Reading

First and foremost, we need to appreciate the complexity of reading. The brain, a magnificent network of neural pathways, is responsible for this feat. When we peruse a text, both our vision and cognitive faculties are engaged. Information is first introduced through our eyes, which is then processed cognitively for meaning and recall.

The brain's two hemispheres contribute to this process. While the right hemisphere is engaged with imagery and visual components, the left hemisphere decodes language and constructs meaning. Reading, therefore, is a cooperative task requiring synchronization between these hemispheres.

Understanding the interplay between the different parts of the brain during reading gives us an understanding of how these processes may be refined and accelerated for speed reading.

3.2. The Importance of Eye Movements

The act of reading involves a complex choreography of eye movements. As we skim through lines of text, our eyes make quick, jerky movements known as saccades, punctuated by short stops called fixations where the eye takes in information.

However, efficient reading is not just about moving the eyes as fast as possible. In fact, one of the concepts central to speed reading is minimizing unnecessary eye movements. Reducing the frequency of both saccades and fixations can significantly improve reading speed.

3.3. Mental Imagery and Reading Experience

When we read, our brain not only decodes the text but also creates mental images. These images play a significant role in comprehension and retention. Speed reading encourages the seamless creation of these images, leading to increased comprehension even at higher reading speeds. This process, often termed as visualization, is fundamental to improved understanding and recall.

3.4. Subvocalization and Its Downplay

As we read, many of us have a habit of 'saying' the words in our mind. This internal speech phenomenon, known as subvocalization, can limit reading speed because the rate of speech is typically slower than the rate at which the brain can process written information.

Speed reading techniques emphasize on decreasing unnecessary subvocalization. By reducing this cognitive 'soundcheck,' a speed reader can significantly surpass conventional reading speeds and yet maintain, if not enhance, comprehension levels.

3.5. Sharp Focus and Reading Speed

The act of reading requires sustained concentration. Practicing speed reading can improve focus and reduce the likelihood of being easily distracted. When a reader's attention is honed, they can process text more quickly and effectively, improving both their reading speed and comprehension.

3.6. The Role of Practice

Just like any new skill, speed reading requires practice. It is during this exercise that the brain learns and adapts to these new methods. Regular practice helps to forge new neural pathways, reinforcing these techniques and making them second nature to the reader.

In conclusion, understanding the brain and its relationship with reading is fundamental to grasping speed reading techniques. By acknowledging what happens in the brain when we read, and how this varies in a speed reader, one can leverage these insights and embark on a journey towards faster, more efficient reading. Reap the multiple benefits of speed reading – a testament to the brain's adaptability and the true prowess of human cognitive faculties.

Chapter 4. Busting the Myths around Speed Reading

The concept of speed reading, as fascinating as it seems, is wrapped in a shroud of myths and misconceptions that often stand as invisible barricades, prohibiting many from even attempting to acquire this valuable skill. Are you one of them? Let's unveil the reality, one myth at a time.

4.1. Myth 1: Speed Reading Means Skipping Words

It's a common misconception that speed reading involves skipping words or skimming through the text. However, this couldn't be further from the truth. Speed reading is about enhancing your reading efficiency, not about missing out on words or information. Techniques such as chunking, where you read groups of words rather than individual ones, and minimizing subvocalization, where you cut back on saying words in your mind, allow you to read faster without skipping content.

4.2. Myth 2: Fast Reading Equals Less Comprehension

The belief that comprehension gets compromised with increased reading speed is inherent but not justified. We all tend to believe that the brain, much like any machine, might not perform well under 'speed'. That it wouldn't maintain its caliber of understanding and retaining information. However, scientific research counters this belief. Studies reveal that as your reading speed increases, your brain adapts to this change by improving its processing ability, thereby enhancing comprehension. Of course, this comes with consistent practice.

4.3. Myth 3: Everyone Reads at the Same Pace

Undeniably, reading speed differs vastly among individuals. Factors such as vocabulary knowledge, background knowledge about the text, focus, concentration, and ability to visualize greatly affect the reading speed. It's essential not to compare yourself with others but focus on improving your own reading capability.

4.4. Myth 4: Reading Word for Word Improves Understanding

Does meticulously reading each word guarantee better understanding? Not necessarily. It may seem logical that reading every single word would improve understanding, but it's not always the case. Our brain has an exceptional ability to fill in gaps and understand the meaning of a sentence or a paragraph even when we don't read every single word. Speed reading leverages this brain ability, allowing us to absorb and comprehend information faster.

4.5. Myth 5: Speed Reading is Only for Geniuses

Perhaps one of the most discouraging myths is that speed reading is a magical skill exclusive to geniuses. In reality, it's a skill that can be learned, cultivated, and refined by anyone willing to invest time and effort. Speed reading isn't about lofty IQs; it's about learning and consistently applying specific strategies and techniques.

4.6. Myth 6: Speed Reading Requires a Special Talent

This myth stems from the belief that speed reading requires a special, inherent talent. However, speed reading isn't a talent. It's a skill and like any other skill, it can be improved with proper training and consistent practice. With the correct set of tools and an open mindset, anyone can master speed reading.

4.7. Myth 7: You Can Become a Speed Reader Overnight

Perhaps one of the most dangerous myths to believe is that you can become a speed reader overnight. Learning to speed read is like undertaking a journey that requires a dedicated mind, sustained efforts, and regular practice. Change, especially one involving our cognitive capabilities, doesn't happen overnight. Patience, perseverance, and training are the cornerstones.

While these misconceptions might shake our confidence, debunking them is the first step towards embracing speed reading. This skill, mastered and applied correctly, can revolutionize your education, career, and overall life, creating opportunities for accelerated learning and expanding your horizons. Bust these myths, and you'll be one step closer to mastering an invaluable life skill on your journey to self-improvement.

Chapter 5. Tips and Techniques for Accelerated Reading

Let's venture into the world of accelerated reading, where you'll discover invaluable techniques and strategies, each designed to turbocharge your reading speed while augmenting comprehension and recall.

Accelerated reading is more than just a skill; it's a powerful tool that can drastically augment your productivity, intellectual prowess, and grasp of critical information.

5.1. Establish Your Baseline Reading Speed

Before you embark on improving your reading speed, you need to know your current speed. To calculate this rate, select any text at a comfortable level of difficulty.

Begin by timing yourself for one minute, keeping track of the number of words you read. At the end of the minute, record your existing word count. This figure represents your words-per-minute (wpm) speed – your baseline reading speed.

5.2. Understanding Your Reading Process

Take a moment to visualize your reading process. Note that your eyes naturally make small, jerky movements (saccades) from one fixation point to another as you read. Your brain then constructs meaning from these chunks of text.

Understanding this fundamental mechanic can propel your reading acceleration journey, allowing you to fine-tune your eye movements and neural processing.

5.3. The Art of Minimizing Subvocalization

One impediment to fast reading is subvocalization - the tendency to (silently) pronounce words in our minds as we read. While this habit aids in understanding the text, it can slow down your reading speed significantly.

Work on suppressing this inner voice to a minimum, allowing you to process textual information visually, rather than audibly. This adjustment will drastically improve your reading speed.

However, be aware that complete elimination of subvocalization can hamper comprehension. Find your balance, and bit by bit, you'll witness the blossoming of an evolved reading speed.

5.4. Chunking Text

The idea here is simple: instead of reading word by word, you read several words at once. The average eye fixates on a cluster of 6-9 characters during normal reading. By expanding these areas of focus, you'll read in 'chunks,' each representing an idea or concept.

Practicing this skill will require patience and focus. Initially, you might feel a dip in comprehension, but with consistent practice, your brain will adapt to this new reading style, and comprehension will considerably improve.

5.5. Improving Eye Movement

Efficient eye movement can significantly enhance reading proficiency. Avoid unnecessary eye movements; focus on jumping from one chunk to the next, reducing the number of regressions or backward glances.

Also, make sure to reduce eye fixations. Most readers have the habit of looking back over a line they've already read. Aim to reduce this habit by diligently practicing moving your eyes forward.

Developing these skills might seem daunting initially. Remember, progress is gradual but absolute if you persist.

5.6. Speeding Up with Skimming and Scanning

The techniques of skimming and scanning are powerful add-ons to your accelerated reading toolkit.

Skimming involves a quick overview of the text to grasp the gist or the main ideas. This technique can be approached by reading the headlines or the first sentence of each paragraph. It's an efficient way of understanding the gist of a text, especially useful when you're sifting through large volumes of information.

Scanning involves quickly looking through the text to find specific information or keywords. Since you're not reading everything, you can move much faster. It's important to know the exact information you're looking for before you start scanning.

Remember, the key to both techniques is a keen eye for details and the ability to focus amidst an ocean of words.

5.7. Train for Comprehension and Retention

Speed reading is not just about fluttering through pages in a jiff; it's about comprehending and remembering what you read at an accelerated pace.

Spend time analyzing the structure, flow, and purpose of the texts you read - this conscious engagement builds a robust understanding while enhancing recall.

Consider charting or mapping content, employing memory strategies like linking, pegging, and using mnemonic devices. Regularly testing your understanding and recall will also go a long way in strengthening these faculties.

Remember, releasing pressure to understand every minute detail aids in grasping the broader concept, so don't be disheartened if some details elude you initially.

5.8. Practice, Practice, Practice

It's important to note that achieving a swift pace in reading isn't an overnight phenomenon; it requires consistent effort, determination, and, importantly, practice.

Start incorporating these techniques into your everyday reading. Use these techniques separately at first, then mix them up according to your comfort and necessity.

Try reading a diverse assortment of materials, as differential content stirs the brain in various ways, further enhancing your cognitive capabilities.

Learning requires perseverance. Your improvement may seem slow at first, but remember each step takes you closer to your goal.

Remember, the journey to accelerated reading is a marathon, not a sprint. The real victory lies not merely in reading faster but in empowering yourself with the ability to learn and absorb knowledge effectively and efficiently.

By integrating these tips and techniques into your reading habits, you are instantly optimizing your time, retaining more information, and redefining your learning capabilities as you familiarize yourself with the revolution of speed reading.

Chapter 6. Pivot: Standard Reading to Speed Reading

In the world of reading and learning, stumbling upon concepts such as Speed Reading can feel like unearthing a hidden gem. It gleams with potential, promising to radically redefine one's cognition and information assimilation process. But to turn the promise into reality, one needs to understand the pivot from traditional reading models to speed reading.

6.1. Going Beyond Traditional Reading

Traditional reading cultivates a linear approach. We learn to read each word individually, from left to right, top to bottom, and one page after another. It's a time-tested method, but it does not meet the demanding pace of the modern world. While it is a necessary foundation, aiming for speed reading requires unshackling from the confines of this standard approach.

To make the pivotal shift, consider the traditional reading process as grist for your cogitative mill. It's an intellectual endeavor intended to extract meanings and deepen understanding, not just a mechanical activity of sounding out words. This transition might be challenging initially. Nevertheless, with consistent practice and a receptivity to adapt, it is feasible.

There are a few crucial strategies to graduate from the conventional reading model:

1. Eliminating Subvocalization: Sounding the words in our head puts a speed limit on our reading. To read faster, learn to understand words as you see them, without vocalizing them

internally.

2. Harnessing Peripheral Vision: Your eyes can perceive more than just the word they're focused on. Use this to cast your visual net wider, reading multiple words or even a whole line in one fixation.

3. Reducing Backtracking: Going back over text is a common habit that slows you down significantly. Strive to understand and assimilate the information in one go.

6.2. The Magic of Chunking

'Chunking' is a cornerstone in the edifice of speed reading. Based on a theory in cognitive psychology, it groups smaller individual bits of information into larger wholes (or 'chunks'). This process enhances information comprehension, memory, and retrieval by reducing cognitive load and increasing the efficiency of information processing.

Mastering chunking involves a few crucial steps:

+ Get comfortable with reading groups of words together and gleaning their collective meaning.

+ As your prowess grows, attempt larger 'chunks' – from pairs to small phrases, and eventually whole sentences or even lines.

+ Train your eyes to focus on the middle of a 'chunk' and use peripheral vision to see and comprehend the remaining words.

6.3. Eyes – The Drivers of Speed Reading

The human eye and its ability to move rapidly are fundamental to speed reading. Therefore, understanding and working on your Eye

Span, Fixation, and Eye Jumps is vital.

+ Eye Span: It's the number of words your eyes take in at one glance. Gradually increasing your eye span can help you ingest larger word chunks and enhance reading speed. + Fixation: It's the momentary pause of the eyes when they stop moving and focus on a text section. The objective is to decrease the number of fixations by expanding your eye span. + Eye Jumps: They occur when your eyes move from one fixation point to the other. Improve this by increasing fixation times and reducing the number of jumps needed to read a line.

6.4. Practicing Well – The Key to Speed Reading

Indeed, practice doesn't make perfect if done incorrectly. On the other hand, thoughtfully planned and well-executed practice sees you reaping the fruits of speed reading.

+ Balancing Speed and Comprehension: Speed at the cost of comprehension defeats the entire purpose of speed reading. Start slow, maintain the comprehension level, and then gradually increase your speed.

+ Use Speed Reading Tools: Several digital tools can help you practice speed reading. These applications enable you to read one word at a time at an adjustable speed, assisting you in increasing your reading speed.

+ Set Regular Goals: Set realistic, tangible targets for your reading speed and comprehension. Aim to clock more words per minute every week. Remember, consistency is critical.

The pivot from standard reading to speed reading is an invigorating journey. It's akin to learning to run after mastering walking; it is the same fundamental process but executed faster and more efficiently, saving time and enhancing productivity. With persistent practice coupled with adherence to the strategies and tools discussed, you are sure to witness a formidable rise in both your reading speed and comprehension levels. Remember, success in speed reading, like any worthwhile endeavor, won't come overnight. But the investment in time and effort promises a pay-off in productivity that will significantly influence your professional and personal life. Enjoy the journey!

Chapter 7. Boosting Comprehension: Strategies to Absorb More

Speed reading isn't just about perusing text at an accelerated pace; it also involves absorbing the crux of the information. Balancing speed and comprehension is a fine art that can be learned and honed. The following sections will provide extensive strategies to boost comprehension while speed reading.

7.1. Developing the Right Mindset

The journey towards increased comprehension begins with developing the right mindset. Remind yourself that reading isn't a chore, but a pathway to knowledge. See each text as a trove of information waiting to be uncovered. Abandon negative beliefs, such as "I'm a slow reader" or "It's difficult for me to remember details." Replace these with positive affirmations, like "I can read quickly and understand deeply" or "I can remember details vividly and for a long time."

7.2. Focus and Concentration

Improved comprehension while speed reading requires intense focus. Fewer distractions lead to higher mental absorption. Ensure a quiet, serene environment before you begin reading. Switch off all digital distractions. Make use of tools, such as noise-cancelling headphones or earplugs, if required.

Mindfulness can boost concentration and retention. Try deep-breathing exercises before you start reading as it helps to calm the mind and improve focus. Remember that reading isn't a race. Give your mind the tranquility it needs to process and retain the information.

7.3. Active Reading

Active reading increases absorption and memory retention. Engage with the text, question what you read, draw conclusions, and make predictions. As you read, continually ask yourself, "What's the author trying to convey?" Thus, you're converting passive reading into an interactive process.

Underline or highlight important points as these aid in revising the material later. Sideline your doubts in a separate notebook, and return to them later for analysis.

> [NOTE]
> Don't let your doubt disrupt your speed reading session. Maintain the momentum, and revisit the uncertainties later.

7.4. Chunking: The Art of Grouping Words

Chunking is a technique where you group adjacent words together into a meaningful phrase instead of reading words individually. By taking in more bits of information at a time, you can read faster and improve overall comprehension. Practice is the key to chunking, start with grouping 2-3 words, then gradually move to larger chunks.

7.5. Using Context Clues

Contextual clues enhance your comprehension ability significantly, helping you infer meanings of complex or unknown terms from the surrounding text. This relieves you from frequent dictionary lookups, maintaining your reading speed.

7.6. Breaks are Important

Never underestimate the power of rest. Continous reading can burden your brain, leading to poor comprehension. Take short breaks after certain intervals – a method derived from the Pomodoro Technique. This technique recommends a 5-minute break after 25 minutes of focused work (or reading, in this case).

7.7. Previewing and Reviewing

Before you plunge into speed reading, preview the material. Scan through headings, subheadings, or bullet points. This act forms an initial understanding of the text.

Also make reviewing a habit. After reading, skim through the highlighted points or summary to reinforce your memory.

7.8. Note-taking

```
[IMPORTANT]
Note-taking is a powerful tool, enhancing comprehension
and memory.
```

Don't just transcribe the text verbatim, but rephrase the information in a way that's meaningful to you. This active engagement with the text helps cement understanding and recall.

7.9. Visualization

Transform those words on the page into a vivid mental movie. Visualization reinforces memory and understanding because our minds remember images more effectively than words.

7.10. Reading with a Purpose

Having a clear purpose before reading helps focus your mind on relevant information. The purpose could be as broad as "get an overview of the topic" or as specific as "identify the author's viewpoint on climate change".

7.11. Speed Reading Software

There are numerous apps and software designed to help you accelerate your reading speed while maintaining comprehension. They use various techniques like rapid serial visual presentation (RSVP), guided reading, and Meta guiding.

Implementing these strategies, with practice and patience, can not only increase your reading speed, but also significantly improve comprehension. As the adage goes, "practice makes perfect"; and with these techniques at your disposal, you can conquer the realms of speed reading while absorbing the essence of the text.

The art of effective speed reading lies in the balance – a balance between the speed of going through the text and the ability to understand and retain the information. The strategies presented here are not merely theoretical concepts, but practical tools to help you on your journey towards masterful speed reading and knowledge absorption.

Chapter 8. Befriending Retention: Remember More from What You Read

The ability to fully retain and recall information from the text you read is a critical component of speed reading. While speeding through content might allow you to consume more information, the real mastery lies in being able to remember and use that information. This chapter will delve into techniques that can help reinforce memory and boost your retention.

8.1. Understanding Memory and Retention

To enhance our skills of retention, we first need to understand how memory works. Memory is often divided into three stages: encoding, storage, and retrieval.

Encoding is when you interact with new information, storage is retaining it over time, and retrieval is accessing the information when needed. To remember something, you have to successfully traverse all these stages.

Several common obstacles can interfere with these memory stages. Distractions, stress, and lack of attention can play a significant role in hampering our encoding process. Equally, our storage process can be disrupted if we do not revisit the information regularly. Failure in retrieval often occurs due to poor encoding and storage.

8.2. Techniques for Better Retention

To overcome these obstacles, it's crucial to develop techniques that streamline and enhance each of these stages. Below are some great strategies that can be incorporated into your speed reading practices to help boost retention.

1. Active Reading: Actively engage with the material. Ask questions, predict outcomes, and summarize the contents. This active involvement can significantly enhance your understanding and retention of the material.

2. Highlighting: Use a highlighter to mark the significant points or anything you find interesting. This activity further engages you with the text and helps to encode the information more deeply.

3. Visualization: Imagining the information in your mind's eye creates mental images that help reinforce the memory. This technique is especially effective when reading conceptual, abstract information.

4. Use Chunking: Chunking refers to breaking down information into smaller pieces, or 'chunks'. Our brains can more easily digest and remember information when it's presented in smaller, manageable chunks.

5. Mind Mapping: Use this visual note-taking method to represent ideas and their relationships. Rooted in cognitive psychology, mind maps allow you to structure, categorize, and visually represent the information, which aids in better encoding and storage.

6. Revisiting & Spaced Repetition: Regularly review your material. Spacing your repetitions helps you strengthen memory traces, leading to long-term retention.

7. Mnemonics: Develop mnemonic techniques that translate information into a form your brain can retain. Acrostics, acronyms, rhymes and imagery — all these can be a fun way to

boost retention.

8. Self-Testing: Test yourself on the material. Self-testing is a highly-effective active learning strategy and can significantly improve your recall.

8.3. Fostering a Retention-Friendly Environment

Understanding the need for a healthy, conducive learning environment is vital for retention. Here are some factors that need to be considered.

1. Optimized Setting: Ensuring a calm, quiet, well-lit, and clutter-free space can boost your concentration and reduce distractions that impact the encoding process.

2. Regular Breaks: Our brains need a rest between intensive bouts of learning. Incorporating regular breaks ensures our brains have a chance to reset, digest the information, and prevent overload.

3. Nutrition: A well-nourished brain is key to good memory. Omega-3 fatty acids, antioxidants, and B-vitamins are known to help with cognition and memory.

4. Sleep: A significant amount of memory consolidation occurs during sleep. Ensuring you get a good night's sleep is crucial for information retention.

5. Exercise: Regular physical activity boosts blood flow to the brain and can help maintain cognitive health, including memory.

8.4. Applying Techniques According to the Nature of the Content

Of course, all reading content isn't the same, and different material may require you to adjust your strategies. Academic or professional texts may call for closer reading, more frequent breaks to ponder over complex ideas, and more extensive use of note-taking or mind-mapping. On the other hand, leisure reading might permit more extensive speed reading techniques, with less emphasis on retention.

In conclusion, the mastery of retention lies at the heart of successful speed reading. With the understanding of memory and the application of the right strategies and practices, you are sure to substantially enhance your retention capabilities. By conscientiously applying the techniques, optimizing your environment, and adjusting strategies per content type, you are setting yourself up for success with speed reading and, most importantly, comprehension and recall. Regular practice and persistent pursuit of these strategies are what will truly yield remarkable results.

Chapter 9. Speed Reading in the Digital Age: eBooks and Beyond

In the exciting new era of ever-increasing digital content, the capacity to read quickly and comprehend effectively not only enhances productivity, but also implicates keeping pace with the rapid advancement of knowledge. Yet, speed reading, traditionally associated with physical books, may feel somewhat restricted when it comes to its application in digital platforms. In truth, speed reading in the digital age cannot only be incorporated seamlessly, but is increasingly becoming integral in the face of digital learning resources like eBooks, online articles, and academic PDFs.

9.1. Entering the Digital Reading Landscape

We begin by familiarizing ourselves with the digital reading landscape, which has seen exponential growth in recent years. Digital books, popularly known as eBooks, have pushed the frontier for readers across the globe. Laden with convenience, portability, multi-device compatibility and environmental benefits, eBooks have become the preferred choice of many modern readers.

With digital libraries, online literature platforms, and open-source academic journals, digitization has led to the democratization of knowledge. A plethora of resources can now be accessed at the tap of your fingers, further highlighting the need to absorb this widely available information faster and more effectively.

9.2. Understanding Differences Between Physical and Digital Reading

The mechanics of reading on a digital platform are subtly different from reading a physical book. Traditional speed reading techniques like skimming, chunking, minimizing subvocalization, and using a pointer may pose slightly altered challenges. Reading a physical book involves turning pages and holding a sense of tangibility whereas a digital platform requires scrolling or clicking to view more content. The difference in the medium of text presentation calls for a revised approach and a slightly tweaked skill set for speed reading.

9.3. Mastering Speed Reading Techniques for Digital Content

To optimize speed reading for digital text, let's focus on leveraging technology's potential in tandem with traditional speed reading methods:

- **Adaptive reading**: Digital mediums allow the reader to personalize font, size, background color, and brightness. By experimenting and finding your optimal reading setup, you can enhance both speed and comprehension.

- **Utilizing eReader's facilities**: Use features like search, bookmark, and dictionary lookup to navigate quickly through your eBook. These features minimize the need to reread, back-turn, or keep external reference materials handy, contributing to speed reading.

- **Chunking**: Just like physical books, the concept of chunking implies reading groups of words together. With practice, your mind can grasp the gist of multiple words in a glance, significantly boosting read speed.

- **Controlled scrolling**: Using the scroll feature responsibly prevents losing your reading flow. Too fast scrolling might make you lose context, while too slow can stifle your reading speed. Find a balance that suits your pace.

- **Minimizing distractions**: Set your device on Do Not Disturb mode while reading. Use Reader View on browsers to avoid ads and pop-ups. A clean, distraction-free reading environment tremendously helps in speed reading.

9.4. Speed Reading Tools and Apps

In the digital age, numerous tools and apps can accelerate your speed reading journey. Rapid Serial Visual Presentation (RSVP) is a method where words in a text are displayed in succession at a fixed point, allowing you to read without moving your eyes. Tools like SpeedReader, Spreeder, and AccelerReader are integral in providing RSVP-based reading methods.

Other helpful apps include Reedy, ReadMe!, and Outread. These offer various speed reading methods like Guided Reading, whereby an indicator moves across lines to guide your eye movement and control pace. By using these digital technologies, you can break free from the limitations of your natural reading habits and infuse your capabilities with the power of speed reading.

9.5. The Role of Practice in Speed Reading

Like any other skill, speed reading with digital content calls for constant practice. Gradually increase the pace of reading, experiment with different tools, and remain consistent. Incorporating speed reading into your daily routine, such as during commute hours or free time, can also prove beneficial. Try to also occasionally test and measure your progress, using online speed reading test resources.

9.6. In Conclusion

Speed Reading in the Digital Age is a dynamic skill capable of transforming your learning curve. By embracing eBooks along with a slew of digital platforms, backed by the right strategies and technologies, you open up a spectrum of opportunities for bolstering your reading speed, comprehension, and overall learning experience. Embark on this journey and witness how speed reading can revolutionize your intellectual progression.

Remember, the whole point of this endeavor is not merely to read faster, but to read better. After all, efficiency is about minimal effort and maximum outcome. On the highway of digital literature, speed reading is your vehicle towards a future that understands time is precious and knowledge, limitless.

Chapter 10. Real-world Applications of Speed Reading

The world today is flooded with information. Books, articles, emails, reports, and more demand our attention and time daily. To keep up and avoid being overwhelmed, it's essential to have a powerful tool, like speed reading, to help efficiently process this information. Speed reading doesn't only help us consume material faster, but it can also greatly improve our comprehension and retention rates. More than just a tool for personal growth, it has numerous real-world applications that we'll delve into in this chapter.

10.1. Preparing Students for Academic Success

In the academic world, the ability to read quickly and effectively is indispensable. Textbooks, research papers, and study materials are all part of a student's routine. A student with speed reading skills is set to succeed in this fast-paced and information-loaded environment.

Speed reading reduces the time students spend on textbooks and notes, leaving more time for other valuable tasks like creative thinking, problem-solving, or even much-needed rest. The techniques also improve recall and understanding of the content, which adds up to better exam results.

Furthermore, in a post-secondary setting where quick processing of academic papers and large amounts of text is the norm, speed reading techniques provide a competitive edge. Using these skills, students can stay on top of their coursework, perform more in-depth research, and engage with the material at a deeper level.

10.2. Enhancing Professional Efficiency

In a professional setting, speed reading can unlock unprecedented productivity levels. Emails, reports, and memos crowd the typical working day and can slow productivity to a crawl. In the face of such information overload, speed reading helps to streamline these tasks and minimize the time spent on processing written information.

Knowledge workers, like analysts, researchers, and lawyers, who must digest and understand vast amounts of text data for their jobs regularly, benefit directly from speed reading. By using these techniques, they can scan and absorb complex data quickly, draw conclusions, and make informed decisions faster.

Likewise, business leaders, managers, and executives, who often find their inboxes inundated with reports, policy documents, and financial statements, can stay on top of their work by embracing speed reading. It also facilitates better interaction with information, allowing for timely responses and informed decision-making, which is crucial in today's fast-paced business environment.

10.3. Empowering Entrepreneurs and Innovators

Next to the realm of entrepreneurship and innovation, speed reading shows its versatility. Aspiring entrepreneurs, who must grasp a wide range of subjects to kick-start their ventures, stand to gain significantly from this skill. From market research reports to regulatory documents and contracts, speed reading allows them to absorb information rapidly, learn from it, and apply it to their ventures effectively.

Similarly, innovators researching new ideas, technologies, or industries can use speed reading techniques to rapidly acquire and apply knowledge. Through speed reading, they can quickly scan through the vast sea of information available, freeing up more time for ideation and creation.

10.4. Promoting Lifelong Learning and Personal Growth

Speed reading isn't solely for academics or professionals – it's a skill useful for everyone yearning for personal growth and development. For those hungry for knowledge and always seeking to learn more – whether it's a new hobby, a subject of interest, or global news – speed reading is invaluable.

With these techniques, a person can enhance their lifelong learning journey by reading more books, engaging with diverse content, and expanding their knowledge horizons. It assures the enriching experience of learning is not time-limited and fosters a growth-oriented mindset.

In essence, speed reading is a transformative skill set that has far-reaching applications across academic, professional, entrepreneurial, and personal spheres. Its utility in more effectively processing information, improves not just reading speed, but also comprehension and retention. Adapting to this approach stands at the center of the future of learning, promising a more informed and productive future.

Chapter 11. Stepping into the Future with Supercharged Reading Skills

In the rapidly advancing digital age, an efficient reading skillset proposes a direct impact on personal and professional growth. Through this comprehension of speed reading, one could harness improved retention rates while significantly reducing the time spent to absorb new information.

11.1. Understanding the Science Behind Speed Reading

Reading is a complex neural process. When we are reading, our eyes discern the symbols (letters), compile them into words, which our brain then comprehends into contextual information. Traditional reading can be likened to a laborious walk, where each word is a step that requires individual attention and effort. Conversely, speed reading is more akin to an effortless jog, where words are processed in chunks, rapidly advancing through sentences and paragraphs.

The central concept of speed reading revolves around two primary factors: fixation and saccades. Fixation is the period your eyes pause to gather information, and saccades are the rapid eye movements in between fixations. Speed reading encourages wider fixations and fewer saccades, leading to a streamlined and swift reading process. Scientific endorsement of this reading prowess substantiates the success rates of speed reading techniques.

11.2. Developing an Efficient Speed Reading Routine

To develop a supercharged reading skillset, one needs to follow a systematic and iterative process, aided by habitual practice and continuous assessment. Below is a guide to help you kickstart your speed reading journey:

1. Discard Subvocalization: It's a common practice to 'speak' the text in your mind while reading, which severely hampers reading speed. This habit can be tackled through chunking (grouping words) and using your finger to guide your reading.

2. Use a Pointer or Tracker: Our eyes inherently follow moving objects. Wielding a pointer (like your finger or a pen) allows better focus and pace, reducing the chance of regression.

3. Prioritize Comprehension: Understanding the material is superior to simply reading it swiftly. A good speed reader doesn't sacrifice comprehension for speed.

4. Gradually Increase Reading Speed: Challenge yourself by progressively increasing your reading speed. This practice facilitates enhanced neural response to text input.

5. Always Warm-Up: Our eyes are muscles that need warming up before a strenuous activity, much like any other muscle. A warm-up can include simple eye exercises or skim reading before you delve into serious speed reading.

6. Regular Breaks: To avoid mental fatigue and sustain reading performance, it's necessary to take periodic breaks. A well-rested mind will always provide a superior comprehension rate and memory retention.

7. Practice: A consistent exercise routine with a variety of texts is vital to enhance your speed reading skills. Over time, your reading efficiency will improve.

11.3. Advantages and Potential of Speed Reading

With ample exercise and persistence, speed reading offers numerous benefits, including accelerated information processing, increased reading stamina, improved memory retention, and above all, a remarkable saving of time.

Contemporarily, where 'Knowledge is Power,' speed reading empowers individuals to stay at the top of their intellectual game. It gifts them an ability to assimilate abundant information in a limited time, from reading a hefty report minutes before a meeting, to cramming a semester's material the night before an exam.

Furthermore, world leaders and CEOs often attribute their success to their swift yet comprehensive reading ability, claiming it to be a vital contributor to their impressive knowledge bank and decision-making prowess.

Indeed, developing supercharged reading skills can establish a future marked with efficiency, productivity, and intellectual superiority.

11.4. Concluding Thoughts

Developing speed reading skills might initially challenge your conventional approach to reading, but the convenience, efficiency, and the vastly improved knowledge absorption that ensues is worth every bit of the effort.

By embracing speed reading, you will be enabling a future rich with knowledge and the power to adapt in a rapidly changing world. The skills learned transcend beyond professional benefits; they're life skills that add value and quality to your existence. Thus, stepping into the future with supercharged reading skills is more than just a shift; it's an evolutionary leap, enabling you to absorb knowledge like never before.

As this chapter closes, remember that the journey towards proficient speed reading is a marathon and not a sprint. It requires consistency, patience, and understanding of your reading behaviors. But rest assured, when mastered, it will fundamentally redefine your relationship with reading, helping you take control of your time and knowledge like never before. Embrace this revolution and unlock unparalleled intellectual potential!

9 798854 915915